MY HEART AND SOUL

MY HEART AND SOUL

By
Marilyn Randall

Personal Touch II Designs by Marilyn
Whidbey Island, Washington

First edition
First printing
Copyright 2009

Lulu Publishing
LULU.com

Copyright page © 2009

ISBN 978-0-557-08757-0

MY HEART AND SOUL

is a sampling of thoughts and feelings that encompasses important events
of my sixty three years on this earth.

My faith is secure and when my spirit soars with cosmic energy
pulsing through every vein, sometimes with such force and deep emotion, I am
compelled to grab paper and pen
and allow it to flow through this conduit of natural body freely and the result
you'll read on the following pages.

Many directions has my life taken, each with wonderful events and others with
difficulties unimaginable,
but today is the better part of my entire life
and I am intensely grateful
for the opportunity to share this part of me with you.

Recently I have been led along a new and unexpected journey. One that is
exciting and fulfilling, nurturing and inspiring, thus
the title of this book
and I dedicate this to the man who has become
MY HEART AND SOUL and THE OTHER HALF OF ME.

My tribute to him and to us is COLORBLIND.

CONTENTS

My Heart And Soul 1
Colorblind 5
From God To Me 9
Now Turns The Tide 11
An Angel On My Shoulder 13
All Of Me 15
For This Moment 19
With Love To Me 21
By The Grace Of Dreams 25
Mornings Glory 27
Shadowland 31
Sister Of My Soul 35
My First Love 37
Timeless Hope 39
Masquerade Of Racism 41
The Brightest Star 45
Truth Of Courage 49
Far Beyond Forever 51
Wildflower 55
My Precious Joy 59
For This My Whidbey Island 61
From A Daughter To Her Father, With Love 65

Peace	69
My Broken Promise To Me	75
Another Question, Another Time	79
A Prayer For Strength	83
Mother	85
Today	87
Kaleidoscope	91
Give It Way To Keep It	93
Bridge Of Hope	97
Broken Circle	101
Even Until The End Of The World	105
Come Play With Me	107
Fusion	109
He Is Mine And I Am His	111
The Other Half Of Me	113
Today's Farewell Is Tomorrow's Prayer	117
A Crystal Drop Of Dew	119
For Peace And For The Children	121
A Love I Have Not Yet Known	125
Better Than Beyond --you	127
To Serve You, Lord	129
I Am Ready	133

MY HEART AND SOUL

Beginnings come so few times in life,
Times to start anew with renewed spark and vigorous
Excitement as spent in youth with love like sap
Dripping from the maple tree
Then warmed by and nurtured to fullest essence.

And times when we are just who we have become
After life has had its way.
Older, more mature, and ready for the door to open once again
And show us life,
For we are young yet in heart, and the time is ours.

Beautiful love of future for what we thought gone
And thought at times to never find again to give us hope
And keep us young,
Knowing not that he was there and did the same
And that soon I would meet him.

Walk through that door and see his face and read his heart
And fall with abandoned want for him
And for the man he became through struggles.
I am humbled by the honor here, and yet the thrill of new,
Both of touch and of caress for him, is wanting.

There I am, wanting him with all of me, and he is wanting me,
And life has painted gray what was not
And set the wrinkles for all to see those times traveled across
The brow in furrowed lines of promise lost,
But I am young again and free, and best lies ahead in the future.

He brings me joy in thought and smiles to crease my face,
Sunshine to my day when his voice caresses my mind.
I love him and best he knows now.
Best he know he is in my spirit and my heart forever soon,
And never again will I be alone without him.

One soul traveling on this journey. Now together after love
And for love, and all of love and joy between us,
The dream came true, for he is real and whom I have longed for
And waited for and hoped for
Again and again. And there he is, and I love him now.

The love returned in passion and tenderness and ways
Of unimagined bliss, and joy before not known
Is in my heart for him and for all he gives me and I give him,
Matter not the distance, for there is none.
Two open souls meld into one, my dearest love, for each is yearning

And wanting to rush til we can be that part of each other
Only dreamed of til now.
The weeks, the days, the hours, the minutes
Rush us toward the edge of life and all we find anew
And all we find lasting and fulfilling this time.

And I can say without a caution that I love him and want him
More every minute to share my life and world.
When life becomes our playground,

Lasting through the rest of all our time,
A time when pasts are gone, when he is all and I am loved.

When raindrops sing against the roof as he loves me,
And quiet places just for us become our safe
And pleasured world where others cannot find us
And he fills me with him,
Then we will have the world and all that was meant to ever be.

No other in this or other place
Ever knew the last of this serene joy, for we will make it even more
And all that it can ever be with us together
Against the world and for the world because he loves me,
And I give him my heart and soul.

COLORBLIND

Swirls of anger settle over me like a shroud,
Spewing their hatred and no mercy for the color of him
And not the man inside.
Protect me from myself and them from me, for I am angry,
And yet I cannot fathom the reason they are blinded.

Beside me he walks, and I beside him, just for him.
And they see only difference where we see same.
Forgive the temper raised within my soul for him, so that I might
Settle difference better than before
And not carve the chasm deeper.

Can't they see the love he offers me and how we are together?
Do they hate? For what reason? And how can it ever go away?
We are the same, an entwined soul of love and gentle caring.
And they cannot see, for they see only black and white and no
more--Only what they do not understand.

Not enough to be so by themselves.
Not enough to spew the hatred for a man because he is dark
And wants one of theirs,
Matters not the kindness and goodness of him.
Yet they would let her go to hate and anger of their same color?

Where is the justice for the suffering he endured?
Where is the penance for the abuse he witnessed?
Where is the punishment for what we did to him so long ago?
We speak of justice, but see it only for ourselves
And not for those who have suffered most

May God forgive them before the end and lead us better than before.
It won't change now and will take forever for some,
But if they look a little deeper they will see:
He gives me what I need, and he is what inspires me to be me.
And to want him is to want my heart to beat.

Softly and gently heal the one who is suffering.
Take the blinders off and see inside his soul,
For better men have not walked beside me and never will.
And yet others cannot see because they are so blinded
And full of prejudice, caring not for truth.

God made life and breath for us all, yet we have damaged part of what
He laid upon our hearts, without hatred.
We told God He wasn't good enough because our image,
Differently seen, is not the same color,
And so we can still worship what? God's mistake for naught?

I think that I have journeyed down this path before.
That I saw the man ahead of me, beside me, and behind me.
And I know they didn't speak and find his heart, but I did.
And I loved it as God blessed it and me for the togetherness.
And thank God I am colorblind,

Or I'd have missed him and who he is.
And so will they. And their loss will be so great.
For kindness he is, and gentleness he is, and love he is,
And I am wanting us and him, and I will not walk away from him,
But I will walk away from them who are blinded.

My loss will be great but theirs is greater.
My loss will be filled by him and all he brings to me.

And what they have left
Is bigot thoughts and empty hearts
And knowing somewhere they are deeply sinning against the God
who is love.

Speak not to me of love while taking from him his rights.
Speak not to me of fairness and abuse while beating his soul.
Speak not to me of same while seeing only difference.
For you are liars and cold as ice, and the hatred burns my heart
As it will yours in Hell.

But enter into ease with soft-spoken words of heart and soul.
Let him show you what he has shown me.
Read his thoughts and tell me it isn't true
Or that he has no caring of me.
Tell me you are colorblind, and yet I will know the truth.

For I see it in your eyes and hear it in your voice.
I witnessed the look of fear and misunderstanding so long ago
And still see today the child trembling with fear
For being who he is,
And I am sickened by the sight of you.

But not just for him am I longing now,
But for all of them and us to lay down the sword and join hearts
And be one with each other.
For they can also look this way and wound,
And we must now enter new and all be colorblind to see.

FROM GOD TO ME

My tortured alcoholic soul
Creates demons the normal drinker cannot see.
A bondage broken, escaped I'll be
When God's loving lessons are learned by me,
And only God can set me free.

For in myself is a growing strength
And the courage to finally see
That no man can take what I don't give
Nor give to me what I long to be.
For only God can set me free.

I search for peace and serenity
After years of pain and agony.
The child inside will laugh with glee,
Freedom will again come to me--
When I find God, He'll set me free.

A child again I long to be,
Naïve, trusting, cherished, and free,
Trading sick and old, tired and weak,
And mortal men to do for me,
For only God can set me free.

And through God's eyes, I will finally see
The abounding beauty of bird and tree,
Of flowers and mountains and frothing sea
And new beginnings made just for me.
And only God can set me free.

And with God's words I will speak to thee,
Wanting only what you can share with me.
Through you His words will come to me,
And I'll be free.
And only God will keep me free.

A lesson of life learned well by me
Is God's blessed gift that will keep me free.
Look back, I can't or I'll not see
The wondrous journey ahead of me,
Expecting not what I cannot see.
For today is here for me to be,
And only today God set me free,
And I have glimpsed serenity,
And truly feel God's love for me.

Thank you God for my sobriety.

NOW TURNS THE TIDE

I grind pebbles beneath my feet
While pounding high upon the beach,
And let not the water touch my feet,
and wash this feeling from my soul,
For now I am absorbed in me.
I cannot bear to turn my face
At any cost myself in place.

The words I'd heard from others, though,
Were humbled words, but not from low.
With graced surrender, this they'd found--
Their pebbles well placed upon the ground.

The moon grows full.
The sand shifts.
The wind blows steep.

A cold shudder fills me,
And now turns the tide..

I bow my head to take my blow.
Ego, self, my need to show:

I want no more that I have been.
I walk the sand to sea.

And so the tide is turning..

My might is gone, but strength I've found
To look to others, to help their needs.
For if not they want, then nor shall I,
And for myself, my highest high.

Surrender to Him, walk with Him,
Follow Him, and heed His word.
Self, I shall not carry now
Or plague myself with doubt and pity.
The light shines from reflecting sea
And bathes my feet in lifted spirit.
For God saw fit to honor me
With grace to Him I'm humbled.

And now turns the tide..

AN ANGEL ON MY SHOULDER

An angel sits upon my shoulder,
Whispering secrets of life's sweet dreams.
And when my body feels burdened,
He lifts my heart, or so it seems.

My angel helps renew God's glory
And the awesome love He has for me
With a wonderful, glorious, loving story
And visions of heaven and eternity

My angel taps me on my shoulder
And guides me through life's perilous paths.
He points me in the right direction
And keeps ol' Satan from my back.

O' stay with me forever, Angel,
And keep me solid in light of day
And cuddle me to sleep at bedtime
With encouraging words you've come to say.

Please stay with me forever, Angel.
Lift your wings and bugle high.
Keep my chin and eyes toward Heaven,
And never let my heart deny

That I might praise in wondrous spirit,
The gifts from God that He's bestowed.
And Angel never let me wonder
To whose loving debt for this is owed.

Lowly would I speak without you.
I need you by my side each day.
Tapping gently on my shoulder,
Keeping me from where I'd stray.

And as this day comes to an end,
From on my knees I pray
For truth to come from an Angel's touch
To all mankind today.

Thanks to you, my little Angel.
Thanks to God for sending you.
Thanks to Jesus who died for me
That I might live my life anew.

May you always delight in the freedom of God,
And may your Angel guide you gently through
This mortal life.

ALL OF ME

The black hole of cancer stealthily crept into our lives.
That ugly C word of dread
That carries with it fear upon the hearts of us all.
Cancer-- the beginning of the end.
And there is no returning from this journey
Or changing what is predestined
By Him who knows all
And decides all.
And then he was gone.

And now it's time to let him go
And go on living as I know
He would want me to do and would do himself.
And yet I hesitate,
For I am saddened at his loss and the loss of being needed.

And I will always wonder if there will be more
Or another who will fill my life.
I gave him everything.
For many years he was my focus,
And now he is gone.

And here I am, left with thoughts and memories,
Unfulfilled dreams and work unfinished.
All the times we had to love and didn't
And no more again,
For he is gone.
He died and so did my heart,
For a time.

Time now to live again,
Breathe again, and be again,
And hope that someday there will be more to this life
For me
To share with someone I could treasure
And be devoted to
And this time love with abandoned heart.

Who would care for me
Enough to do for me what I did for him once,
And love me deeply as I need?

Devotion--
The newest word I've learned,
More than love, more than loyalty.
Devotion for a day, a year, or a lifetime.
I can do that again for him,
For someone new,
And yet I dream of more.

No regrets,
Only loss and yearning for something gone
That I hope will come again, even better.
And yet I would do it all over and over
For another someday
Who would do the same for me
And who needed me,
But I long for more than need today.

The black hole of cancer stealthily crept into our lives.
That ugly C word of dread

That carries with it fear upon the hearts of us all.
Cancer -- the beginning of the end.
And there is no returning from this journey
Or changing what is predestined
By Him who knows all
And decides all
And then he was gone.

FOR THIS MOMENT

And in the magic of a moment, there you are,
Just the thought that you noticed me, and my heart is racing.
The sound of your voice and I am trembling.
It must be you: no other has this affect upon my heart.

You were gone so fast before, left without a word.
Will you leave again like the passing of a cloud or stay this time
To hold my heart and mend my soul and take me
Where no other takes me? It must be you.

Tall, young, beautiful, can you really be a part of my life?
Or do you want something I can't give you?
Make my heart sing and my body breathe with yours.
Two in sync like the wind and the sea. It must be you.

Even for a little while, let me have that part of you.
Let me soar with you as you soar and carry me away
To places only we know about where others cannot find us.
It must be you because you are the only one I want.

All of you, if only for today. Let me ride your spirit and your soul.
Take me, baby. Make me young enough to hope
And feel enough to take you to the top with me.
Give me you. Give me to you. It must be you.

Don't let go. Don't take away my heart and drop it.
Keep me safe and take care of me, even for a minute or a passing few.
Take me with you, baby. Come to me baby,
And let me love you better than before. It must be you.

Follow me, lead me, talk to me, and whisper dreams of love to me.
Touch me, hold me, caress me, just never let me go.
Let me be the one you love and want better than the others
And always with this passion. It must be you.

WITH LOVE TO ME

From the darkened caverns of my soul,
Secrets from a distant past
Torture me with the horrors of
Ancient feelings blinding grasp.

I can heal from deep within.
Cast out blackness from my mind
And tell the truth and ask them all
To only treat me thus in kind.

Revealed the truths from childhood
When fear gripped my every day.
When sweat ran off my brow in slumber,
When they came to me to have their way.

The truth I tell now, once forsaken,
Not hiding in death's shadow still.
Enough of empty hollowness
That this hurting should now be revealed.

Enough of power that they had
To have control of me.

My Heart And Soul

I want me back. I want to live.
I want forever to release,

The ugliness within my mind,
The pain of no relief.
In sun there's shadow, always shadow.
In darkness, fretful, restless sleep.

Never free of who they made me.
Never can I shed inside
The torment of the deepest valley,
My soul intent there to reside.

With truth I know now who I am
And know where lies the blame.
I was the victim of abuse,
And in my mind was thus insane.

Today there's hope of bondage gone.
Thank you, God, for my today.
With grateful heart I look to you
To release me from these binding chains.

I need your help to feel again,
To rid me of these walls.
I have survived within my body,
But my soul has been in its vault.

If now my walls won't crumble down
And I'm left imprisoned in my past,
I will not feel my love for me
And others' love has not a chance.

Replace my fear with gentler ways.
Let me renew my hope and wonder.
Help me heal the pain inside,
And keep me from peace no longer.

I now must let them go away.
You know the truth of who I am.
I am a soul who has found at last
Freedom from the lost and damned.

Forgive them, Father, and please help me,
As in life I now begin to grow
To pray for those who long ago
Held captive my tortured soul.

Please help my heart to open wide
And swell with newfound love,
As I begin to love me now
And always look to You above.

BY THE GRACE OF DREAMS

There was a moment, a fleeting thought,
Streaking through this life without fear,
Following moonbeams and starlight and gently
Replacing reality with fantasy
And guiding me through yesterday and tomorrow.

One thought, then another, and then gone.
Replaced those quiet times and golden memories
Shared before and yet not again.
Be gone, for darkened shadows lurk,
And one is very real for me this time.

I am frightened lest it be forever, and I stay.
Take me back to whispered love and quiet corners.
Let me feel the nearness of the Angels once again,
The soothing music of our dream,
And share the gentleness of soft sweet breast with me.

Never will the sight of God be there, but here.
All His glory keeps me safe and holds me firmly in this place
Of soft, pale clouds,
Feathered gently between layers of my scattered mind.
He watches from afar and waits. Be gone.

For one day I too will have to go there,
Rescued not from darkening shores and thundering sky,
Waiting for the gentle touch of your hand to pull me out
Of muck and mire from whence I came.
Take me home now and let it lie forever gone, away from me.

Tomorrow's dawn is brighter with the passing memory of that dark.
And let future sail pleasant and serene,
For he still waits. And I still run the other way,
Through every door away.
He finds me not yet, and I am peaceful and at rest until it begins
again.

MORNINGS GLORY

With a solid loving attitude,
A new day for me has dawned.
Today to make a memory.
Tomorrow to look back on.

Tomorrow's birth will be a memory
Only the day after when
I look today for happiness
And place it well til then.

A pleasant time my mind shall make
And then relate to you a story
As I anticipate the dawn today
And appreciate morning's glory.

The sound of dawn is silent
As earth swirls to break of day.
What excitement stirs within me
As I anticipate a way

To live the fullest every minute
Of this day God gave to me

To experience all the wonders,
To see all there is to see.

Then birds trill a morning greeting
As sunlight bursts to light the dawn,
While clouds dance across the ceiling
And its for me to carry on.

I snuggle closer to your warmth,
This day will wait no longer.
These thoughts will be for us to share
As through the day I wander.

I might walk along a sandy shore
Or hold a child's hand.
I might climb a craggy cliff
Or try to do all that I can.

I might catch a fish for supper
Or maybe take a ride with you.
I might write thoughts in a letter
Or find a friendship to renew.

I might smell flower's breath today
Or cook a hearty pot of stew.
I might soar high in an airplane
And then make tender love with you.

I'll not be disappointed
At whatever the day shall bring.
I'll take whatever comes my way
And thank God for giving me

Another day to witness life,
Another song to sing,
Another night turned into day
To see what life might bring.

No matter what the memory
I make today, it seems
It wouldn't matter at all to me
Without you to share my dreams,

So once again I thank you, Lord,
For loving me today
And also for the love I've found
Beside me as I lay.

Thinking of a morning's glory
And all that it will bring
And all we share each day we have
And all our lives now mean,

And now with loving attitudes,
A new day for us is dawned.
Today to make a memory,
Tomorrow to look back on.

SHADOWLAND

The Shadowland of wasted life
With souls cast into Hell,
Where I have been for most my life,
There in the drink I dwelled.

Shadowland, the land of dreams
That never quite come true.
And always myself within the shadow
Of the drinks I've paid in dues,

Dreaming days of wasted time
And on a bar stool, there I am.
Remembering how it used to be
Before I didn't give a damn.

And now a shadowed soul of yearning,
Craving and alone at end,
Only drink to soothe the timeless agony
Of drink, my only friend.

The screaming in my brain relentless,
From withdrawal the nerves are raw.

My Heart And Soul

These tremors uncontrolled in shadow,
And more drinks for this I sought.

One drink poured down to stop the shakes.
These hands with no control,
My throat now burning, I swallow fast,
Liquid gold to soothe my soul.

This drink I need, but I don't want.
I can't stop the need for more
To fill the brain with false euphoria
And kill all my life for sure.

In morning's light I see not the dawn
Or brightness of glowing sun.
I reach for drink from where I lay,
In Shadowland of burning rum.

I've sold my soul before for spirit.
I've sat on the corner curb
And shared another's last drop of flavor
And thought not of the other's words.

My body is old now and failing fast,
The stench of death seeps from my pores,
The shakes return with agony
As my brain screams out for more.

Oh God, help me! My soul is lost,
Given freely for one more swallow,
The night chill fell as I barely move
In this Shadowland where I wallow.

A drink I need so desperately,
But there is no more of me to sell.
And life is but a stagnant memory,
As it became this living Hell.

Once, when I began this journey,
The drink brought joy and laughter.
Those days of merriment, so long gone,
Left with Shadowland forever after.

Lord, I don't know what's wrong with me.
It's what I want no more,
But something's broken and snapped inside,
And for me there is no cure.

This living death of no emotion,
Only thoughts to find a drink.
Until my churning instincts find it,
There is nothing more to think.

Then yesterday appeared an Angel.
He's with me still today.
He wiped my brow throughout the torture
As last night turned into day.

I made it through without the drink,
And as we pass the hours this day,
He's kneeling here beside me now,
Helping me learn how to pray.

You, God, will bring me some relief
And save what's left of me to save.
He's talked to me of newfound hope
And helped me make it through this way.

What's left of me shall never be
The best I could have been,
But, Lord, if you will help me now,
I'll do with it the best I can.

This man you sent to guide me
Talks of just one day to me.
He tells me if I turn to you,
From the bottle I'll be free,

With You to guide me and lead me back,
I have a tiny speck of hope.
Thank you God for wanting me
And sending him to help me cope.

I am such a lowly servant, Father,
An alcoholic tortured by the need of drink,
A miracle yet to be alive,
So brain damaged and slow to think.

From Shadowland, where I have been,
Where there is no relief,
To you I'll turn now in my pain
And walk to you from tortured dreams.

The Shadowland of wasted life
With souls cast into Hell,
Please, Father, help me to be free
And need not the drink with which I fell.

SISTER OF MY SOUL

My sister Sherryl, who lies deep within my heart,
Is not of blood, but of this life, for she is real and shares
With me this life and time and joy and love of life,
Never holding back, or hurting me along the way.

Truth and honor for the sober days ahead,
And years we now know were passing like gentle breezes,
Yet swiftly moving in search of resting,
For God came first, and they cannot take those times away.

Times we spent in search of life and sober life.
Laughter shared and love and growth of self.
Always being there together for each other,
Sometimes away, but always in the heart.

My treasured friend of years and years
Who taught me of her life and then shared mine.
Forever strong, yet I learned the gentle
Caring of her ways and held her fast as she did me.

She wiped my tears and I did hers,
Always sharing love for God and others

And this newness of ways to see and breathe and live
For something different than before.

No more the drink to kill the pain, and
Only joy of new learned skills
And trust in God this time, not others,
But in Him, the force of wholeness and peace.

Sister, you grace the world.
You took me in and taught me so and then you let me fly.
You are my treasured heart forever more,
And I am blessed that God saw us together,

And I am blessed to know you and have you,
My dearest friend, who knows me too.
Inside my soul and life and quiet gentle places,
We reserved for only just the two of us, always.

I love you, my sister. You are my friend, forever.

MY FIRST LOVE

Shining sunbeams warm the surface and settle colored glows
On mountain meadows filled with fern and dancing flowers.
Blessed they be for blooming now beneath the winter's white caps
And over Spring's dampened furrows
And hidden stones.

Blankets stretching far over dale and under ridge
Where we walk beside each other, hand in hand. And then
We'll share the dream of night and day again,
Together strolling, being one with all around
In His gracious place

And loving God and all He brought us to,
For in His image, we'll be blessed to wander far and see inside the heart,
With each a map to follow and path to walk as soon again, we go,
For ours is now and Heaven is only there
When we decide to search.

These pulsing hearts will be with us forever and never go
To places far away, and yet they keep rapid beats to soar above the earth
While Angels trumpet like the eagles cry, as climbing into clouds above,
And then try again to match the altitude
With fearless glides on singing wings.

God's place of worship for those in awe of him and all His wonders
Set beside the meadows and the brooks for us to blend and become part
Before the love that moves our hearts to one
And back to Him in perfect love
As He made for us.

Beneath the shelter of the leaning tree and veil of rustling leaves,
You love me with the heated passion come to pleasure each,
And just for us we are alone with glory and peace in His kingdom,
Sharing deeply of this early natural wonder
Between man and woman.

Our place remembered with promise today, like it was only yesterday
And not a hundred years ago. Never does it change, and my heart yearns for you,
As it always has, and that glorious place beneath the sky and upon the bed of fallen leaves
He gave to us that day to take upon our hearts
And never give away to anyone again.

And I have carried all of it, for all these years, and only now return to see the place.
I return to watch and dream again where dreams were born and bodies one,
In His wondrous world where we loved each other and left each other after,
Never to return except in spirit and mind
And dreams of another time.

My first love, never lost until the end.

TIMELESS HOPE

Do I dare hope someone will care about me again and maybe find me a little attractive and special after these years that have left me a little battered?

Do I dare hope to feel that little tickle of excitement in my tummy again when he walks into a room looking for me?

Do I dare hope he'll want to touch me, kiss me, and hug me until I see stars, and will he see more of who I am on the inside rather than the outside?

Do I dare hope to have someone in my life that I can cherish for just who he is today and who might do the same for me?

Do I dare hope for someone I can feel safe with to share my most intimate thoughts and who will be open and trusting enough to share his with me without thought of judgment from either of us?

Do I dare hope to feel that magic inside my heart again when he smiles at me with that twinkle in his eye?

Do I dare hope he'll awaken that sensuality in me that has been so long buried?

Do I dare hope there is someone who will see beyond the gray, the wrinkles, or the few extra pounds that life has laid upon my hips and who knows that true passion comes from a place so deep that one cannot see it, but can only feel it?

Do I dare hope for someone kind and considerate to want to be in my life today and to want to share with me both the joys and the pain this life has to offer?

Do I dare hope that after all these years of life he will now be my soft place to fall when the outside world gets tough and that he will be my rock when I need someone to lean on?

For whatever time I have left, do I dare hope to love and be loved better than what I had in my youth?

Do I dare hope he will be my hero?
And do I dare hope that I have become the kind of person that I yearn for so that I can do the same for him?

If God grants me another chance to share my life with someone, let me honor him, treasure him, laugh with him, and love him without reservation or fear, and let me be equal to what he offers me. Let me show him that I am worthy of someone like him in my life today.

Yes, today I dare hope.

MASQUERADE OF RACISM

This life now merged, one with another as we walk together
And venture down life's path as one.
Always together, forever in future,
Reaching back only for memories, not really wanted now,
But needed reference for the future times and questions asked,
So that we might reveal the masquerade of racism and prejudice
We experience each day we walk within the crowds.
Our hearts are so full of love for each other,
Yet wary of the inequities amongst others towards us,
And between them.

Why do they not understand the injustice of their sightless sight?
Why do they have such deep prejudices in their souls
And hate for another
And such disregard for the raw emotion of a man?
I cannot fathom not loving him and they do not understand,
And continue to see only difference, and not same,
Where same lies so deep.

Do they not see the goodness he is or the greatness he is?
Do they not see inside him as I do and do they miss
Most of who he is because they cannot see beyond
The color of him?

He is good and true and kind,
With all the qualities I have longed for in my life,
And together we are a perfect blend
Of color, of sameness and of harmony for each other.

Yet they shun him and now me.
Where is the justice?
Where is he supposed to go to be cared about
For who he has become and the man he is today?
He is a better man than most who claim to be better,
And are not.
He is a bigger man than most who claim to be bigger,
And are not.
He brings an insight into life,
Unmatched by those who know better and don't.

I know the heart of the skinhead and I tremble
At the prejudice and injustice within.
I watch the good ol' boys and I see the skepticism and hatred,
Be it for a woman, a black, a gay or a Jew.
They think they are above and will never be beneath,
And that no one is better than they are,
Nor near their equal.
I have experienced the mentality of the, save yourself,
White male who thinks he is always right.

I have suffered at the hands of the redneck
And the abuse of the white male who hates women
And cries foul when she abandons her own for others who are kinder.
We are all seeing the brutal Taliban and extremists
And where their abuse of women has taken them.
For how long are we going to tolerate this in our own society,
Under the mask of racism and hatred,
Where soon there will be no difference, than we now see,
In extremists throughout the world?

They are always better, never wrong, and always in forced control,
Because to loosen the reins means to loose,

And they will die before they loose.
Now they push their agenda further, to include
Anyone who is different than they and who they cannot control.
And today they just plain hate.
Always that ugliness,
Just around the corner, under the rock or inside their head.
Hatred for the difference with no understanding of compassion from within.

How honored I am that we are one with each other.
That he is with me today, walking side by side.
He is my adored one, my truest love.
If I should loose him, I would die of wanting ,
Because we are so right together.
I will always fight the battle for us,
For the sameness and the love we share,
And our right to be together in peace, without concern or worry.

The march towards the elimination of prejudice
Is a slow, trudging trek through miles of evil smelling bile,
And years of hot volcanic ash, erupting from hearts, heavy with hate.
They are always waiting for someone to trip and slide
Face first into their Hell as they continue to march and fight for death
And spew their rhetoric and hatred just for the color or religion of another,
Who is different or believes different than they.
How dare they spread their vulgarities and how dare we
Accept them and say they can't be stopped?
When do we stand up and say enough and forbid any more
Of this obscene behavior in our society?

We stand on the hallowed grounds of future and we can change.
We stand on the shame filled grounds of past and we have to change it now.
We have generations of this behind us and God forbid,
We have generations of this ahead of us, without change.
For our children's future and our own peace,
The masquerade of racism has to be unmasked, once and for all.

And it is a masquerade and a dance of difference and indifference.
A misguided roll into ideology that is insane and futile,
And must be stopped to be made right again,
Or forever we will be lost.
This greatest generation of the world has just one shot
To make it right.
And this time, we can't afford to miss.
Take off the mask and be yourself,
And feel the joy of the love between us all.
Stop the dance of indifference and join in the march for love.
Stop the masquerade of prejudice and racism and join humanity,
And know the gentleness and peace God wants us to know,
And the elusive serenity that we all know is waiting,
Just behind that crippled mask of hatred.

THE BRIGHTEST STAR

The night is still, the stars shine bright,
But one outshines above.
It is the star to honor Him
Who came to teach us love.

The star shines on to guide the ones
Who want the words of truth.
They bring the gifts their people sent
From far around the earth.

Three powerful Kings, who journeyed long,
Brought gifts from the world afar
To look upon and worship Him
Who lay beneath the star.

The humble shepherds also came,
Silent as the lamb.
Their only offering was their faith
In this baby God sent to man,

Wrapped snug in common swaddling,
He is who they have come miles to see,
This tiny babe in Mary's arms,
The King of Kings is He.

Angels hark with trumpets high
For Christ this night is born,
Proclaim for all the world to know
With music from your horns.

Sing forth they did of this Virgin Birth.
God sent His only Son
To save mankind from mankind's fate.
Praise Him, the only one.

And in the manger of filtered light
And lowings heard by few,
The Christ Child born in Bethlehem,
God's word has just come true.

The star is but a lasting symbol
Of that night when He was born,
And brightest did it shine for us
When the Angels played their horns.

If your walk through life seems filled
With troubles along the way,
Praise Him who suffered most,
Give glory to His day.

Remember when the worries come
That God did love us so,
And He gave to us His only Son
Who suffered that we should know.

The way with Him brings peace for all,
And others shall find their way
To give their love to all mankind
As we celebrate this Christmas Day.

The words of Christ still lead us,
And even though we stray,
Through Him comes our forgiveness.
Praise Him in every way.

Please celebrate this day for Him,
Remembering long ago
The Baby Jesus God gave to us
To ease our troubled souls.

The night is still, the stars are bright,
But one outshines them all above
It is the star to honor Him
Who still teaches us to love.

TRUTH OF COURAGE

Of courage I have seen it willed.
Witnessed purge from deep inside
Darkest caverns of memories past,
Spewed out with freedom's strengthened cast
Like lightning striking dying pride.

Honest truth to heal the soul
Heaps mounds of glory with God's will.
His helping hand and grace for not,
Aching pain relieved, yet not forgot,
And soon the empty hole with love to fill.

Spent forth on others and swallowed up,
Inside a life through eyes is seen.
Joy, the treasure sought with care
And humbled now to others share.
Prepared, the soul washed new and clean,

And courage was the missing key.
Not courage of power, but of truth
To free the troubled mind and rest.

My Heart And Soul

The heart is quiet, and now its best
Will be for courage and it's proof.

Of happy years and woe no more.
Rigorous work to know in me
I too can share the freedom of
The purge of gore and bring it up.
True courage, pain, and then I'll be

Free, my God, to share what's best in me.
And lies no more to me I'll share,
But honest searching each day I live
And give the best there is to give.
Gentled now with courage to care

And give what's best in me.

FAR BEYOND FOREVER

Oh bother me of past with thoughts
And dreams that do not last
Of make-believe and fantasy
And visions of the past.

Try, oh heart, to stay here now
And clear my muddled head
From demons lying side beside me
On this lonely, restless bed.

If I am here, I cannot weep
For pleasured ghosts who moan and creep
And haunt my tainted life of past
And keep me from a restful sleep.

The sleep beyond these caverns walls
I yearn for slumber from.
And rest and peace with renewed life
Past guilt of living gone.

My Heart And Soul

Far beyond forever
There exists the righting of the winds,
With muffled voice and vibrant light
An endless love begins,

Begins to grow when He is first
And shelters, then adores,
Those searching for the burdens
Cast off from life before.

Folly gone and truth beginning,
Embraced of His gentle touch
Within my heart, He's always been there
And given oh so much.

With need, when I reached out my hand,
Then looked to Him above,
Reminded then with precious peace
Of abounding and eternal love.

And far beyond forever when
He calls me from this life,
My heart will weep no more in mourning,
Ripped open, charged of strife.

Glory of His word always
When from then I'll seek no more.
Far beyond forever
As I walk through His open door.

And rest in peace, my soul gone home,
And memory left troubled life.
They'll weep of lost yet glory in
His way of love, not death's respite.

Far beyond forever,
A treasured, gentle place to dwell,
For greater glories than now I know
Or those other voices tell.

And far beyond forever,
With His Angels there, I'll hold tight.
The dream that God's true love for all
Will dwell forever in my sight.

WILDFLOWER

When the wildflowers grow in spring,
So shall I be there,
In meadows, or in forest romp
With blossoms in my hair.

A barefoot nymph, I'll tread the path
That before me they have gone
And wander through the meadows vast
And take you now along.

There's color pushing through the softened earth
And a bursting from the forest floor,
Past damp and dark of winter's cloak
As sunlight warms the earth once more.

I pause to wonder where they've been,
And why for short duration
Their brilliant smiles of lifted face,
This beauty of God's creation.

They decorate the mundane scene,
A splash of color here and there.
These wildflowers by the flowing brook
With fragile blooms so very rare.

My Heart And Soul

I've trudged the hilly mountainside
And found them underneath the trees,
Protected by a soft mossy blanket
Or a cloak of last years fallen leaves.

Color--glorious color everywhere.
So perfect, each stem and shape.
Buttercups like spreading honey
Or the red bells by the country gate.

Or trilliums under fronds of fern
In woods found near the shore,
Scattered amongst the sheltered shade
Like an artist's palette on the forest floor.

Pinks are rich and snuggled close,
Like velvet covering the ground
And valley's bobbing heads of lilies
As wind whispers quiet sounds.

In drier mountains of rustling pine,
Even there the blossoms grow,
And pungent fragrance fills the air
with mock-orange found not below.

I've seen them bunched near a weathered post
Of a broken down old fence
Or picked them by the handfuls
From the meadows where I spent

Those summer days of freedom,
Romping the weeks away
While wildflowers bloomed on a climbing bank,
Barely clinging to the clay.

I've seen birds-bill scattered beneath madrona
Cat's ear and lamb's tongue too.
And occasionally a delicate lady slipper,
Dripping with drops of morning dew.

Fields of wild, white daisies grow
Higher in mountainous meadows
Where I'll pluck the petals for to tell
The love of my special fellow.

The bleeding heart, in shades of pink,
Will nod its sad and sleepy head
While buttercups blanket a field of yellow
Next to bells of deep blood red.

So take not for granted the beauty here
As we wake from Winter's rest,
The most colorful sight in all the world
As wildflowers spring forth in zest.

And when the wildflowers grow in spring,
So shall we be there,
In meadows or in forest romp
With blossoms in our hair.

Barefoot we will tread the path
That before us they have gone
And wander through the meadows vast
And take others now along.

MY PRECIOUS JOY

Precious joy for remembered times,
When gardens bloomed and rainbows filled the sky,
And you were here with me, living forever today
And knowing it was always ours.

And then, in a flash of thought,
The sweetness of your presence was gone,
Gone forever and never to return.
You died that day and so did my heart and soul

And the will to go forward without you.
But God revived me somehow, and sweet memories I am left
And live for quiet times when I remember
Precious joy and all of you.

He took you home too soon.
My light dimmed in space, and my heart stopped beating
As I lost sight of your soul.
He has you now, not I, and I am heavy with the loss.

I will the light to return to the stars so I can see your eyes again.
The sweet smell of you to fill my head and the taste of you
To return to my heart,
Just to remember your precious joy.

The twinkle in your eyes again would bring me back to life.
The last words spoken as we parted fill my memory with love
For you and for what we had together.
And then He took you from me,

Like a thief who raided my entire life.
Without you, my joy is ended, and your journey is now without me,
And that was never going to be—never.
And yet it did, and my love is gone with you.

Forever I carry you tucked in a tiny corner of my heart
As I release you to Him and regain myself,
But it is the hardest time for me.
My precious joy is always you, and now it's forever gone,

Except that sweetness left to me of memory,
Like a soft warm rain and a gentle breeze that whispers love,
You are my precious joy, and I miss you.
God, why did you need her more than I?

She was my life, my breath, and my heart.
All the joy I felt in a day was her and who she was.
Care for her greatly until I get there,
And her precious joy will always remain mine.

FOR THIS MY WHIDBEY ISLAND

O' carry me along the way
Singing softly with the sway
Of footsteps lightly on the sand,
For this, my Whidbey Island.

Where conifers reach to the sky
And great bald eagles soar and fly.
Where seals and gulls are abundantly found
And sand meets surf in the Puget Sound.

Where shells wash up on rocky shore
And God's gifts to me are so much more.
Deception pass where beauty abides
With deceiving swirls of dangerous tides.

Where wind blows steady o'er gray green sea
And billows a sail with the breath of a breeze.
Where men face the challenge with lure and a hook
Of landing a King-- the elusive Chinook.

Where dawn breaks through the morning fog,
Saving silent ships from rocks and bog,
And Double Bluff tells its own story
Where sunsets glow in awesome glory.

Where Native American folklore mysteries
Still haunt the sun-bathed central prairies.
Where Ebby lost his life to those
Who felt his way on them imposed.

Where tall-masted ships at one time sailed
Into bays rich with life, and this they hailed:
The clams, crabs, and bounty galore,
And the splendor of Whidbey's magnificent shore,

Where serenity sought was glimpsed by few,
To only those who somehow knew
That this gift from God was from within,
To cherish this very precious Island.

So carry me along the way,
Singing softly with the sway
Of footsteps lightly on the sand,
For this, my Whidbey Island.

Where great blue herons sail and glide,
Dolphin and whale swim side by side.
Where starfish and dogwinkles play hide-and-seek
And moonshells and cockles are treasures to keep.

Where the baritone voice of the foghorn call
Lulls me to sleep like a cradled doll.
Where the lonely sound of a calling loon
Is heard on the night of a full amber moon.

Where deer graze silent in meadows of grass
And shadows cross cliffs to fully enhance
The magic of night winds, of fog and of surf,
Where clouds race silent above bountiful earth.

I'll take with me from all around
Memories dear that I have found,
And always remember where 'er I go
To recall the pleasures of my island home.

So carry me along the way,
Singing softly with the sway
Of footsteps lightly on the sand,
For this, my Whidbey Island.

And all the treasures God blessed to me
And they were free, and so I'll be
On this, my Whidbey Island.

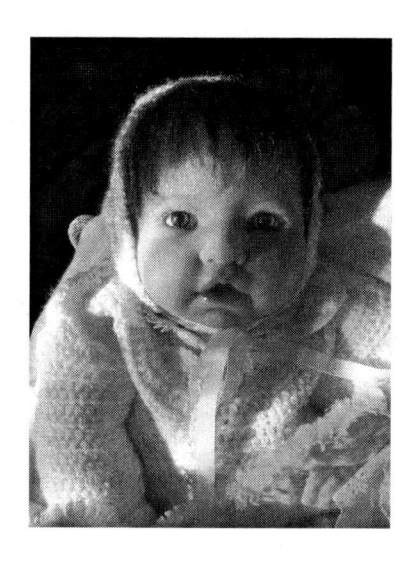

FROM A DAUGHTER TO HER FATHER, WITH LOVE

Dear Daddy,

In all the years we've known each other, I don't think I've ever written a letter just to you. I always wanted to let you know how special you are to me and how much I love you, but the years go by so quickly, and before we know it, way too much time has passed and way too little has been said.

This letter is just for you, Daddy. To thank you for all you've done for me through all these years and to tell you what a wonderful father I think you are.

Do you remember when they first put me in your arms after I was born? I wish I could. I can imagine I felt safe, the same as I do when I think of you today.

My first memory is one I've heard you tell me: I know I was a colicky baby, and I cried a lot at night when everyone else wanted to sleep. And I know you'd put me on your chest where I'd feel safe and warm, and you'd pat me to sleep. You must have been awfully tired some of those nights, but you loved me. Thanks, Dad.

When I think back to the things I can remember of my childhood, I have special memories of you. You rescued me a lot when I was little and even "saved my life" when you pulled me off that electric fence. I remember you were like the sun, warm, full of laughter and love for your family and for me. I remember your sheer delight when I would say something "brilliant" at age eighteen months or walk across the room with a special flair meant just for you, Dad. I delighted in doing something squirrelly that would gain your attention and make you laugh. Remember Daddy?

Oh, you had your "moments" too. Such as the time you pretended to be a bear and growled from the bushes. It was too late when we realized it was you who caused us to make fools of ourselves as we ran for our lives down the gravel road, afraid the bear was going to eat us. And you laughed until the tears ran down your face, and, later, we couldn't help but laugh with you. I also remember when you didn't want a little black puppy for Christmas. Do you? It was the gift we brought you, which we really wanted for ourselves, but we had to take it back to the pet shop the next day. That was a hard lesson to learn, but probably harder for you to teach us.

I grew up with the best memories of a father who was strong, brave, and the most handsome man in the whole world. Did you know I used to sit up nights next to your bedroom door to be closer to you because I knew you would save me from the shadows and the sounds that would frighten me?

I used to miss you terribly when you were away working in the summers, gone before daylight and home after dark, but I always knew I was part of the reason you worked so hard. I always had a wonderful home to live in, always enough food to eat, and special pretty dresses to wear, and I know you made sacrifices just for me so that I could be proud of who I was. Thanks, Daddy!

When the day finally came that I got into trouble, it was you, once again, who helped save my life by having the courage to confront me with love, patience and acceptance. And later, when I came to you with truth that could have destroyed a lesser man, you shared your grief and pain with me, yet opened up your arms and loved me. Your gift of love allowed me to feel that love and to begin my life anew with freedom. You helped me heal by loving me. Thanks, Daddy!

I remember you wanted your daughter to be a lady. Thanks, Dad, for after I stopped "arm wrestling" with the boys, I began to understand the value of being a lady. I hope I make you proud, Daddy, for even though there have been some rough times, I hope you always knew I wanted to please you more than any other person in my life-- just because of who you are.

I wish we could have had more time together because I know I could have learned so much more from you, but the things I value most about myself today, I did learn from you. You gave me honor, respect, humility, loyalty, strength, courage, and love. Thanks, Daddy!

I was right to admire you all of those years. You were, and are, my courage and strength in so many ways. You are the best daddy a little girl ever had. You are also the best daddy a big, grown-up lady ever had. And when I say my prayers at night, I have a special one for you, and I never forget to thank God for having blessed me with such a wonderful father. I will always love you, Daddy, and I will always be your "little girl." Thank you, Daddy!

--Marilyn (1994)

My father passed away in 1999, but not before he read and loved this piece I did for him. I framed it and gave it to him for Father's Day, and he would show it off to everyone who visited him. I will always be grateful that I wrote it for him and gave it to him so he would know before he left us just how special he was to me.

PEACE

And for the Peace,
The perfect Peace,
His perfect Peace.

And His perfect Peace
He brought to us
Through the miracle He
Lived
That each of us would
Know
Of God and all His Holy
Peace.
He became our Savior,
Born of torment and a
Suffering heart.

Born for us to follow,
To learn of hardship,
To learn of walking with
Him
And living for a renewal
Of our soul
While bathed in the light
And warmth

Of His perfect Peace
He brought to us
Through the miracle He
Lived.

We share,
Never being perfect in
Ourselves,
Yet searching to be of
Service
To Him and others.
Yet He continues
Picking us up,
Lost souls and broken
Spirits
And renewing our faith
And hope
That all lives will be
Better
By His touch
And His merciful grace.

His perfect Peace
He brought to us
Through the miracle He lived.

I see the brightness of
His light,
I feel His hand holding mine
And His arm
Surrounding me with the
Warmth
Of His love.
I feel the whispered
Breath of His words
Of hope
Against my face.
Knowing He is always
There,

I follow Him
With love.
He brings Peace to my
Heart,
His Peace,

His perfect Peace
He brought to us
Through the miracle he lived.

Born of Mary,
Humbled by His birth,
And Joseph who loved
Him
And called Him "son."
Joy to them that
Sacrificed

That they should bring
Forth
The Savior of the world
And His Peace
And nurture Him to
Manhood.

Then suffer His loss
Like a blackened hole in
His Mother's heart,
And she prayed
Let Him not suffer long,
My God.
Let Him know You are
There
And receive Him back
From where He came
With love unknown to
The human heart,
And joy and Peace

Be left on earth,
His Peace,

His perfect Peace
He brought to us
Through the miracle He
Lived.

And I shall use Your
Love
To share with all I know
The story of Your birth
And walk on earth with
Others,
Following You,
Sharing Your words,
You left for me and
Others to follow.
Behind You we walk
As we search for Peace,
Your Peace.

Sometimes it comes to
Me
Of loss and sadness
To cry and mourn and believe
I know best for me
And others.
Each time the lesson is
Learned:
That Yours is the only
Truth for man,

For all men,
For every man,
And mine is sated in
Selfishness.
To honor You
Is the only way for me

To know Your precious
Peace.

Your perfect Peace
You brought to us
Through the miracle
You lived.

May I be a tiny voice for
You,
One voice in the chorus
Of the world.
And as we gather volume
With voices singing Your
Praise,
May the story of You
And the Peace You offer
Us
Be the one bright light
That all
Will follow forever,
Loving You.
And may Your perfect
Peace grace the world
For eternity
As each of us searches
Here on earth and in our hearts
For that Peace.

His perfect Peace,
His perfect Peace He
Brought to us
Through the miracle He
Lived.

Amen

MY BROKEN PROMISE TO ME

Promises to me, myself, I make them
And shatter them repeatedly.
Where is the path of glory, God,
I used to think was there for me?

The sweat of blackout just recovered
As daylight breaks with morn of day.
I promise me no more the sickness
Of whiskey downed and life this way.

No more, Lord, this drunken stupor.
From my tangled mind I find the thought,
Fleeting now as again I tremble
And begin the search for just one drop.

Oh God, if You could only find me
And help this wretch begin again,
She'll promise not to drink today
And start this body now to mend.

A promise, God? Yes, it's a promise,
But broken every early dawn
When my brain is screaming for one more
And I begin the search for what is gone.

My Heart And Soul

Whiskey has destroyed my soul
And other parts of me that were within.
There's not much left of me to save now
As I begin that shaky search again.

Stashed somewhere, where no one finds it,
My hidden source for steadied nerves.
Every day relief that comes from
What others call my just deserts.

My leaded heart this night responds
With heavy beats too slow and steady,
Then races with the weight of worry
For again I make this promise empty.

Promises come easy, Lord,
When my body is soothed with booze.
But that won't last. They'll shatter now
From fractured strength of nerves too soon.

Again, each time I'm close to reaching
To you for the help I need.
The misery of abstention suffocates,
And my soul out loud begins to scream.

Promises to me, myself, I make them
And shatter them repeatedly.
Where is the path of glory, God,
I used to think was there for me?

No, never now, for more I need,
My disgusting, hopeless mind recalls.
Within ignited fury I am reminded
Of one more time my hope then falls.

Everyone has given up on me,
Accepted mine as living death.
This trash they see with unkempt hair,
With bloodshot eyes, and wretched breath.

It's all they know now, for I am gone.
The lady just went away.
And all that's left is this broken promise,
Which I break each time my insides beg

For more … more … more!
Another drink, just so I can function.
Then twisted thoughts within me strike
The torment of promises once more broken.

Another slug of whiskey down,
Another empty for the pile.
And with this swallow comes a bit of peace
That lasts for only too short a while.

A promise, God? Yes, it's a promise,
But broken every early dawn
When my brain is screaming for one more,
And I begin the search for what is gone.

Promises to me, myself, I make them
And shatter them repeatedly
Where is the path of glory, God,
I used to think was there for me?

ANOTHER QUESTION, ANOTHER TIME

The emptiness of Heaven's breath above the snow-capped mountains
in distance, and I, left below on soft green meadows, left to wander.
Just wandering, wondering
Where my heart and soul are leading me?

On what journey will my Creator send me this time?
Am I alone?
Walking along this road, visions of memory darting
Through my mind with yearning, always yearning.

For closeness shared, a touch, a kiss, a caress,
And yet I am not sure.
Should the Heavens open up and angels trumpet,
Or is the tenderness enough to pleasure?

What am I searching for, and why is sight elusive?
Do the rapids have to overflow their banks?
Does the ocean have to roar alive with frothing wave?
Do storms have to spend themselves with frightening power

For me to know that what I was searching for is within my reach?
Does he have to be more than who he is for me to know,
Or will his gentleness and passion be enough to carry me
On lifted wings and rainbows evermore, for just who he is?

Journey on this heightened path is lost on me as vision spends
From deep within my breast and pulses quicken at his sight.
Maybe he is the one, but how am I to know for sure?
Where is that list and map and lesson taught before, when I was younger?

Now I have it not and must trust myself, for I cannot again.
These mistakes are mine to make again and again,
Yet do I try to find another way this time?
Does he know me and want me to himself alone?

Questions always questions and answers not yet coming forth.
He asks me, and I know not yet,
For breached is time and journeys longer.
My window here is short, and I must make it right for both.

He asks me when I will know and how, and I cannot tell him.
For somewhere deep inside I ache to know the sureness
Before I leap with abandoned desire, trying to hold dear
To just me.

My wandering and wondering gone now and best I rest,
For breath is gone and sight no longer holds a break through darkness.
Where, my love, are you going, and where am I?
Separated now and forever.

That kiss was true, gentle desire and passion burning softly
That faith cannot sustain, but trueness, then victory, at last.
I am not ready to take the last leap and chance.
True to myself this time, and might he know it now, it cannot be him.

It might never be anyone, and then I'll know the chance was missed forever.

But rather that than this uncertain destiny of self
And life of expected harm and hopelessness again,
And certain unfulfillment made impossible to change.

I would rather die than endure the cage of pleasure for others
And not myself and deny myself my destiny of self.
I would rather die than change a man,
For only with his true self can he ever be fulfilled.

And woe be the woman who missed that lesson and tries,
For her life will be so stained by hatred and resentment
And power that rules and dominates her soul.
But that is not for me this time and only means be true to self,

No matter what the pain, for that is short, then longer life.
Good-bye to dreams, must now be said and told with conviction for his sake.
And ask me not all reasons I have dreamed and thought, but know that reasons were Right and true for self and for him.

Maybe soon, another who fits within my soul and body,
Deep within another journey, begins again together
As we reach for each other, and it is dual and forthcoming by Heaven's grace,
And right this time for both and beyond wonder next.

A PRAYER FOR STRENGTH

On bended knee I ask you, Lord.
To let Your love wash over me as do my tears.
To cleanse me and keep me strong in Your faith,
For as I travel my earthly journey, it's You
Who gives me strength and courage to go on
Searching for the serenity that comes through You.
No matter my travels, my pain cannot compare to Yours.
Let me remember You always and walk hand in hand with You,
Facing the light of Your grace.
Your perfect truth will lighten my burden
And allow me to carry Your message
So that others may come to know of You.
Keep me focused, Lord.
As my path becomes darker and more troubled,
Let me hear the voices of your angels
And reach for the warmth of Your light

And as Your hand gently guides me home,
May I, at all times, be prepared for the journey ahead
And Your loving arms.

Amen

MOTHER

My life came unto me from God, through you, my Mother, and He blessed me dearly when He chose you to bear me life.

God knew I would need a Mother of patience, compassion, sacrifice, understanding and unconditional love. He knew I would need strength and courage, and he knew I would need a never ending amount of love.

You fed me of yourself when I was born. You cuddled me close to your soft, warm body so that I would feel secure in the gentleness of my home. You wiped my drippy nose, washed my dirty face, patched my cuts and bruises, and dried my woesome tears for what must have seemed like an eternity. You fed me, sheltered, taught me, and loved me, until like a fledgling sparrow, I was ready to leave your protective nest and venture out into the world on my own. I've fallen many times along the way, but you never lost your faith in me or your love for me.

A Mother should know that she's done well. She should know that all her trials and sacrifices were well spent and that she is loved by her child for a job well done.

I love you, Mother, for bearing me, for giving of yourself so many times and in so many ways so that I could experience this joyous life that God has blessed as mine today. I thank God every day for the perfect match He made when He chose you to be the Mother for me. I thank you for being the epitome of Motherhood that you are to me.

With loving gratitude for the woman you are. I will always love you, my Mother.

TODAY

Sobriety, the absolute.
My absolute, loving truth for life.

How much love for man have I exchanged for numbness found in golden liquid to soothe unending pain of life's plateaus?

How many memories have I missed for senses blurred and distorted?

How many wasted minutes, hours, days are gone forever that I cannot recover, exterminated by the need of another heavy ounce?

How many friendships have I lost and choices vanished for lack of trust?

How many times have I cursed God for all this pain dealt only to me by this cruel hand and not from my own sick soul?

How many sunsets of colorful splendor did I fail to see lighting up the evening sky with vibrant fury in hues of ever-changing warmth?

How many falling stars did I miss because my eyes couldn't focus for need of more to drink?

How many times have I blamed parents for life's seed that started this and left me always needy and helpless?

Sobriety, the absolute.
My absolute, loving truth for life.

Did I miss the longing of need in another's eye?

Did I miss a child's hand reaching to me for comfort?

Did I miss your call because the ringing in my head drowned out the ringing of the sounding bell?

Did I miss love offered by another?

Did I miss an opportunity to give something of myself to someone else in need?

Sobriety, the absolute.
My absolute, loving truth for life.

Ah, to climb the highest craggy cliff in spirit, a thrilling trip within my mind.

A glimpse of selected daylight for today and then the journey with my imagining soul and sober being.

I no longer feel lost and dead in spirit.

My life soars on feathered wings of dreams and leaves my heart open for messages sent from God.

My eyes are clear of fog.

My mind is healing and is no longer filled with so much self-delusion.

Each day, the light within me glows with joyful celebration for my own creation and for my Creator.

Sobriety, the absolute.
My absolute loving truth for life today is found this day.

This day, this one day, to stay, I pray,
Sober, for just one more day. Today.

KALEIDOSCOPE

In times of silence, there I wander
    throughout my mind and soul.
Searching always for me.
Trampling into dark, hidden corners
    tucked away beneath my spirit
    where I stay for only seconds.
Pain of memory rushes past and I retreat
    to open, lighted caverns full of mystery
    where my spirit flows with joyful anticipation.
Quickly gone as I continue.
Wandering.
Searching always for who I am.

Kaleidoscope.
Imagined beings of truth.
Reality; insanity?
Me?

Filled with delusion, I dare not trust
    for even I can deceive, especially me.
Fantasy? Make-believe?
Wandering.
Always in search of me.

Where did I go?
Was I ever there or here?
Am I a figment of my own imagination?
Is anything real, tangible?
Is this muteness the essence of me?

Who are you?
I don't know if you exist or if I dream you.
The tunnels continue forever.
A maze of disruption, constantly changing.
I may never find my way back.
Back to what?
To what you say is real or what I think is real?

Kaleidoscope.
Imagined beings of truth.
Reality; insanity?
Me?

GIVE IT WAY TO KEEP IT

God showed me the days of my life today,
He showed me my future too.
He allowed me to see where I would be
If I had continued to do what you do.

As I purged my soul for the memory,
I relived my horror of drink,
I spewed out the words of hopelessness.
I forced myself to think.

I walked your path today, my friend,
But I held onto God's hand
To show you the way it has worked for me
And others who've followed this plan.

When I looked into your glassy eyes,
I felt the same despair.
I remembered the agony I once felt
And the destruction that got me there.

God gave me the greatest of gifts today
When He placed you into my life
And allowed me to help show you the way
Out of futility and sordid strife.

He gave us the Big Book to study,
A text of lives before mine,
A way to stay sober together,
Together, one day at a time.

He gave us the twelve steps to follow,
To practice each day that we live,
"Put a cork in the bottle: it's simple."
And learn not to take, but to give.

Give what's been given before us,
To free us of chains of the drink,
When given as best we know how, it's simple,
just "Don't take that first drink."

Practice each step as we know it.
Turn our lives and will over to God.
Allow Him to work miracles for us.
Allow him to be God, who is God.

God showed me the days of my past today.
He showed me my future too.
He allowed me to see where I would be
If I'd continued to do what you do.

God's working for you today now,
For you are His miracle too.
Sobriety--the gift that He'll give
If now you do what we do.

Don't drink, and the rest will follow.
Life changes, and it's on God's terms,
And someday you'll give back the sweet gift of life
By giving back all that you've learned.

Our reward comes directly from God
By doing what He wants us to do.
He'll give back a life of joyous rewards.
It's no longer just up to you.

Today we are working together,
Showing each other the way,
Sharing God's gifts and His love
Makes the difference in our lives today.

We've known the bondage of drunkenness.
Now we're learning how to be free.
We thank you, God, every day that we live,
For our renewed life in sobriety.

BRIDGE OF HOPE

Oh tell me not of fallen bridges,
Lest ye forget to be.
Tell me yet of velvet petals,
Show me tenderness of love to see.

Caress the newborn's tiny head
And blow ringlets from his brow.
Watch his smile of gladdened life
Renew for me like he is now.

Then cry for darkened cavern's stillness,
Hollowed eyes and deadened souls,
Minds that wander yet forever,
Sometimes here then to and fro.

Tell me not of fallen bridges,
Cross born of leaden wood.
Let my soul be free of darkness.
Grace me now with life so good.

Hope therein fills all my searching.
Paths to wander for challenge sake.
Let Gods love fill me with wonder,
And life's cruel burdens let Him take.

Bridges fall and burn tomorrow,
But there I know not how I'll be,
Needing not to care for others,
Days and nights, this day for me.

Oh tell me not of fallen bridges.
The fire of Hell burns very deep.
Hear the angels message for me,
I'm grateful I'm alive to weep.

For others and their deadly toils
And anger fought there deep within,
Taking on self-righteous armor
Strapped to nights of deadly sin.

When crossed the bridge of hope bears
Cast from strength of faith forgot,
Always but a path away,
Yet times remembered, not for naught.

So tell me not of fallen bridges.
Cast me from this inside pit.
The other side is love and light.
In squalor here no more I'll sit

Shackled by my blinded sight.
My heart and soul yearn to be filled
With love and faith and hope renewed
From God, my life will be His will.

I ache to cross the bridge of thunder,
To pass from dark and into light,
Before the bridge falls then forever
Where I'd be bound by sightless sight.

When I pass, then shall it fall?
Not waiting for the rest behind.
Not if acceptance be their shield
And to His love they are not blind.

Always there to love and guide us,
Angels bear the message clear.
Thank you, Lord, Your bridge I'm crossing.
I'm coming, Lord, there is no fear.

Your bridge is strong with proven words.
For truth and love You died.
Your gentle mercy guides my way.
I seek my journey by your side.

BROKEN CIRCLE

Lasting promise from the other world
Always broken at the end,
And hoping this time the promise lasts,
For there is anger in my soul for wanting more
And never finding truth and always searching

For that other part I cannot find.
Can I always keep above the stench of despair?
Keep others from knowing I am in pain?
He didn't have to tell me lies again
For it to end--just truth. And I would listen

And take to heart his meaning and his heart,
But now the chance for that is past and
Lies upon lies he hands me still.
When will I have enough of this and let go
Forever so that I can be well again too?

I want to heal from hurt that sears my being,
Like a torch come to burn away the edges.
He keeps lighting the fire and letting it smolder
And then lets the pain seep deep into me,
And no relief is exactly what he has to do to me,

And shows me his troubled side, sickened by the past.
And taking me always there to punish me,
As he was punished. And now I see
That the circle has to break this time
Before he dies, and before he takes me with him.

Not enough to treat him kindly, as he cannot feel.
Not enough to love him, as he cannot love himself.
Not enough to care for only him, as he will
Always need many to fill him up
And then let them go with pain, as he does me.

And the circle has to break or I will die.
Sucked into the sewers drain and flushed
Like the garbage he thinks I am.
And I need to know I can never change him
Or how he sees the world and me, for I am only I.

And I need to know that he is not the only one
For me and someone kind is there to treat me as I deserve.
I will not be alone, but better that than this.
A sickness I cannot mend or purge alone
Without help from others, and he will not.

Forever wanting just one man to love me, and yet
I feel unworthy of better for I have never had.
My sick side controls the thoughts of him
And brings him back, time and time again.
And now I break the circle for the last time.

And he is gone against my back that walks away,
And I am free to explore and learn who I am
And why I can never do this very thing again.
And I must break this circle and run for my life
Or I will die with him, and I cannot let that be.

It is my life to save and my soul to heal.
No man will ever abuse me again, for I am worthy
And shall fight until I die for freedom and my will
To be filled with love and cherished always.
And tomorrow the broken circle will slowly close around my heart.

EVEN UNTIL THE END OF THE WORLD

Lo, I am telling a story of old.
A story before so many times told.
This time it's different as said before.
This time it's mine, and you it's for.

It's a story of light found only with truth,
A story of hope after despair,
A story of love and loneliness gone,
A story of faith and a soul repaired.

A story of healing my innermost spirit
And coming to know the Son of God
Who came here to save me, forgive me, and love me,
To help me believe what I used to not.

My spirit was broken and darkness abounds.
My soul and heart could no longer be found.
My voice cried to no one and no one came,
Until I finally cried out His name.

My Heart And Soul

I asked God to save me, my heart to mend.
I heard his voice gently say it then.
Look unto me, for I am your friend.
Open your heart, and let me come in.

"I'll never leave you, even until the end of the world."

He'd been there beside me all along, don't you see?
Yet I didn't see Him til my heart ached with need.

Thank you, my Father, for my life that's gone past.
If I'd not had that, I'd not know this.
I needed those lessons and problems and pain
To appreciate, through You, all this I have gained.

May faith, love, and patience be always in me.
May I give to others what's been given to me.
May I hear Your words always through others I know.
May my heart stay open to You and continue to grow.
May I look always to You, never with doubt, nor in fear,

And know that You're with me and treasure so dear
Your words spoken gently for all to hear.

Look unto me, for I am your friend.
Open your heart, and let me come in.

"I'll never leave you, even until the end of the world."

COME PLAY WITH ME

Come play with me in dancing forests.
Let your feet touch upon the sand.
Look in my eyes with yearning wonder,
Never letting go of my extended hand.

Come play with me by golden beaches
And meadows covered in bright pink blooms.
Let not our age cause us to fear,
Nor regrets to alter all that looms.

Youth may be gone outside ourselves
But not inside our hearts.
Keep me young enough to wonder,
And let me always be that part

Of your playful ways and best of friends,
Your lover and all the rest.
And please, dear, mind not the ones before,
But know you have loved me best.

Come play with me in quiet gardens.
Romp with me in trickling streams.
Care for now there is a morrow,
And listen to your childhood dreams.

I thought that never you I'd find.
I thought the passion gone.
I'm blessed again to love again
And feel safe in your caressing arms.

Come play with me, my newest longing,
Then rest beside me as I sleep,
And gently wipe away my tears
If ever I should cause to weep.

Life passed so fast and sometimes hard,
But now again a newfound chance
To laugh and play with renewed youth
And playful days that ever last.

Come play with me for future times
In all the ways we find.
Gently treasure this wondrous love,
And treat each in cherished kind.

As thunder tromps across the sky,
He'll shelter me in kind.
He'll walk beside me when we go.
He'll leave me not behind.

He'll play with me in future.
He'll play with me in now.
He is my heart and treasured friend.
He found me, I know not how.

Our troubled hearts are lifted,
For now we've found each other.
Come play, my darling, if you dare,
And we'll need never seek another.

FUSION

Feelings like no other have I here within me.
Thoughts of you keep pulsing through my mind,
With cravings like an addict in need of a fix.
I want you with me and near me and in me,
Touching me and caressing my entire being.

Keeping me satisfied with the splendor of our love,
New and helpless in your power to possess
This body and soul and keep me just for you.
And release my anguish once more for all of you,
Filling me with your manhood and your passion.

The want of you is burning so deep within all of me.
Thoughts possess my every breath with yearning,
Like a spoiled child who can never get enough
Of everything that only feels like magic inside and out.
You are the power of my deepest crevice, and I want you.

Each new day dawns with splendid thoughts of you,
And every night your imagined touch is the last I feel
Before slumber finally takes me to our place of quiet dreams.
And early then it changes to the fire within my belly
That only you can ease and calm with you,

My Heart And Soul

And once again, I am high on trust for where we go
And how you soothe me and bring me back to gentleness
Where you are and where you will soon lie beside me always,
With more than passion but also the deepest love,
Where the rest of the world is not allowed to enter or know,

Except what we show them with a glimpse of our desire,
As they watch the love smolder between us and know that we are one.
And we have it all, as was given to us by the grace
Of a power so intense, we could not ignore it nor walk away.
Right the world and spin the night with longing, for he is mine.

And I will always walk with him, side beside him,
Proudly seeing only what we share and through our eyes.
It is beautiful and so very real for us, with a power of heat
I never felt from any man before, and I can barely stand
That I have only days until he's here with me,

Until I feel the touch of him, the taste of him, and cradle
His scent in my heart, for only then will I be complete.
And if the pleasure rages now before I meet him,
The fire will explode when once he is in my arms. And I know
As he takes me and becomes part of me and I of him.

Like magnets drawn by unseen power and forces unexplained,
We know we are now fused as one forever, his and mine.
And fires kindled from this glow will heat our life in future,
As always this gift for each other is placed on an altar
And worshipped for the treasure it truly is.

HE IS MINE AND I AM HIS

May the days run together and time be lost on us,
And all the joy in our hearts be shown to the world on the outside,
Like a flag waving proudly in the wind,
As we walk together down this newest path.
He is mine and I am his.

With desire strong enough to withstand critics
And act as a shield against bigots to protect us
From ugly jealousies and words hurled like thrown out garbage
Because we stand together.
He is mine and I am his.

Gods children, inside and out, and a life well lived.
And now it's our turn
To be with the living and throw off the color and difference
And only see the same and be the same, for
He is mine and I am his.

That strong proud man who stands with me and protects me,
Who guides me and leads me,
Who supports my dreams and helps me attain my goals,
And who I lie beside each night, safe and warmed.
He is mine and I am his.

I glow with desire and longing to explore and experience all of him.
My impatience for togetherness sometimes overwhelms me
As I yearn to be with him,
Again and again.
He is mine and I am his.

He completes my womanhood and gathers me into him.
He treasures me and loves me and desires me.
I am loved, and I love in return like no other before him. And I take him where only we
Know of, with the gentle courage only I can give him.
He is mine and I am his.

Blessed are the days together forever
For those who lost it once, treasure it last.
As we show the world our love and cherished longing for each other,
Never letting go or a single second given back, for
He is mine and I am his.

And grateful for this chance
To blossom and live and experience the wonder of him.
And thanking God for this journey and joyous beginning,
Blocking out the wrongs to make it right, for
He is mine and I am his.

Time marks, until our death, the needed steps along the way,
And future builds this house of solid stone,
To protect from harmful winds.
He is my fortress and protector and my hero.
He is mine and I am his.

Greatness of courage spent and life well lived in early times.
Rewards for suffering and pain
And twisted bodies put right again.
For loss and loneliness now gone and love replaced for now.
He is mine and I am his.

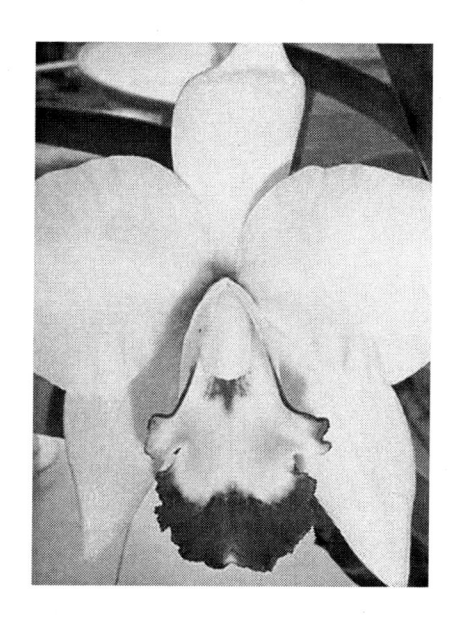

THE OTHER HALF OF ME

The moment flashed again.
Oh memory of times past and loves lost.
Fear and trembling hands of terror held a shuddering heart aloft.
Frightened of darkness and alone and then gone forever,
And now the leap from highest edge to soft, green meadows.

My Heart And Soul

From towering cliffs to quiet streams,
His gentle heart is there waiting, and I am falling now.
Leaping this time, jumping with abandoned,
For life itself has never been so tender or so sweet with taste of new
And never showed me caring like this before.

His arms and heart are waiting to cradle mine to him.
No sharp edges. No ledges of frightened memories,
No wanting more than he can offer.
Just gentleness and kindness, trust and joyful love
For me this time that I deserve.

Protected, loved, respected, and treasured.
Not Cinderella running for her life with slipper lost that night,
But held in esteem and revered for my womanliness.
And he wants me. He wants to be my prince,
He wants to be my hero.

Slowly sliding that slipper on my foot, he holds my skipping heart.
His eyes never leave mine, as he is the truth between us
And lets my soul feel his touch in unimagined ways.
This man of courage gives me tender moments and
Caresses my heart with true kindness and blinding honor.

No care of differences, for none of those we will ever see.
No difference greater than love can cast out.
No difference greater than love can shelter with honor
For who he is and who I am.
Needing not another, only each other, together.

Finally my heart is still and filled.
Not racing. Not yearning. Centered and still
As I watch him come to me, as I watch him want me,
Knowing he is the one to fill me up with him
And always will be.

I gave before. I gave until there was no more of me,
And now he wants to give to me
All that he has in him to give,

All that he has and more until my soul is full.
And I will do the same for him, for my heart has bloomed with him.

And life is centered and, once again, now focused just for us.
I never stopped searching for him. I never gave up.
And then I found him,
And I found the other half of me,
The one I lost so long ago.

I knew not
That he was searching and longing for himself to be fulfilled
With true passion and deep love.
Accepted and cherished for who he is only
And those evasive hearts not yet connected.

And then he found me soaring on the wings of unknown journeys
And wanted to share the life God gave each
With each
And began this day of together
And fulfilled and protected life, forever now and ever.

Black, white, young, old, man, woman,
I care not, for all is whole this day. All is whole and right again.
I found the other half of me
In an unexpected place and way, and it was God and all His glory,
Once again, who knew and showed me how.

TODAY'S FAREWELL IS TOMORROW'S PRAYER

Silent whispers mostly clear.
Vanishing thoughts so quickly gone.
Billowing clouds fleeting with the wind
Whose presence sings of saddened song.

A son that I once cradled near
And now seems forever gone,
A mother's moan of pain and loss,
Yet still the days move on and on.

I watch, with wonder, for memories
Played out in elegant motion.
A thunderous sky retreating not
Clearly the dance of my devotion.

Forever I will carry him,
Those memories precious in my heart.
He made the choice to change the end;
No one can ever change the start.

My Heart And Soul

Within my soul all yearns for calm
And a softening of edges played.
A puff or wisp of white or blue
As harsh memories slowly fade.

God, stay with me and help me heal
And forgive him for his part.
Let me accept Your will this time
That you might ease this breaking heart.

Like clouds becoming fleeting white
Then building toward the sun,
My hopes soar high as do the clouds
Until reality overcomes.

They shroud my life; this canopy,
Spreading thin across the sky,
Played out someday like life in me
When I become too tired and die.

Bid farewell and let him go,
My son, who has gone away.
Great hope of spirit, like dancing clouds,
Stay within til my last day,

And someday before that day comes
I'll see and hold him once again.
For You, God, might bring him back to me,
And I'll forever be his Mother and his friend.

A CRYSTAL DROP OF DEW

The petals fade and fall at last,
Like precious memories from the past.
Timeless aging for just a few,
Reflecting times of me and you.

Our times of youth, adventure bound,
When life ahead was all we found.
We had not yet met with the past.
The past takes years of souls to cast.

My thoughts reflect now from afar
On who I am and where you are.
Our spirits bound by time well spent,
Forever saved, and never lent.

And in the distance only peace
With the grace of God to guide me.
Yet while still here of friendship thought,
The kind we've shared cannot be bought.

My dear friend, I think of you.
Of all those days when we both knew
Our separate ways that we might go,
Yet someday time would bring us home

My Heart And Soul

To know again the joy inside
Of my friend once more by my side.
And all that I can give to you
Is reflected in this drop of dew

That time will never take away
Nor share with others from that day
Of old, when young and bold and few.
Memories reflected in this drop of dew.

So as the bloom fades from the tree
And waves still pound with churning sea,
Reborn is youth in other's child
As the moon glows white, yet not defiled.

And stars dance bright above the earth
For time's relentless renewed birth.
The woods of eons petrified,
And the drop of dew is crystallized.

And our thoughts of love will then endure.
Our spiritual ties, of this I'm sure.
Immortal will our friendship be,
Forever my friend, in you and me.

Memories cast, I give to you.
Reflections in a crystal drop of dew.

FOR PEACE AND FOR THE CHILDREN

Oh desperate child,
Come kneel with me
And feel his presence
Overpower thee.

May He bring you love
In your frightened place,
And may He also bring
The world peace.

The joy of goodness
God passed to us,
The prayers of healing,
The hope of trust.

All are treasures
To be shared each day
And the joy of love
His words convey.

Oh lost little child,
Come kneel with me
And know your Lord
As He is to thee.

May He bring you love
In your shattered place,
And may He bring
The world peace.

Lift your shaded eyes
To the glowing light.
Press your hands to your heart
And cast out the fright.

Oh grateful child,
Come kneel with me
And feel His spirit
Overpower thee.

May he bring you love
In your gentled space,
And may He bring
The world peace.

His life He gave
So we might be
Forgiven our sins,
He knew we'd need.

So pass His joy,
And sing His praise,
And love Him always
In every way.

Oh blessed child,
Come kneel with me
And feel His spirit
Overpower thee.

May He bring you love
In your sheltered place,
And may He also bring
The world peace.

And trust that He,
In all the world,
Will bring lasting peace
With a truce unfurled.

Then sing of joy
Each day we live,
And to the children
Always give.

And may the children's
Suffering ease
When He brings this world
A lasting peace.

And on this joyous
Of all days,
Please trust with hope
As we silently pray,

For peace and for the children!

A LOVE I HAVE NOT YET KNOWN

Tomorrow I will say good-bye to a love I have not yet known,
One that I deeply wanted, yet never found until it was over.
Way too soon it was gone, and the rest of my life I will wonder
If there could have been a forever with you
And if we missed the last great chance to love in this life.

We met long ago, it seems, and yet it was just a blink away,
And time rushed by as fast as the wind on a stormy night.
And all the turmoil of passion grew within us as we hoped
And prayed we would one day meet and share this love, pulsing so
As it has from distance shared, but time took its toll.

And I will say good-bye to a love I have not yet known,
A passion I have felt inside my chest and loins for a man so vibrant
With life and so beautiful with soul. And how I wanted you
To be mine, but as it passed another day, I then knew
It would never be and it could not ever be.

For it wasn't ours to take this time, and we have to go on
And maybe never find this for another. And so the days will be
Heavy and long, for longing and wondering if it could have been.
While I say good-bye to a love I have not yet known,
I am tormented by the memory of passion lost forever now.

Of time with him to know his body and his soul with mine,
To know his heart beating against mine in perfect harmony
And to feel the heat of him within my grasp and his,
And to know the joy and rapture of together with the edge of life,
And then the fall of bliss never to be shared with another.

And I am greatly saddened by the need to leave him now,
Before we will ever know those fantasies made real by time
And deep emotion shared for each other, with each other,
While I say good-bye to a love I have not yet known. And perhaps
Forever we will long for each other in memory of what was not

Meant to be for us and will not be for another.
Just in time to save myself the fall and pain of loss even greater,
I cry out for him as darkness takes my hand, and I miss him.
And I have to let him go again before we are finished with this love,
While I say good-bye to a love I have not yet known.

As tears course down my silkened cheeks and stop they won't,
For I am heaving with the sadness brought by his loss
And time less than when together but longer than before.
And I cannot see him anymore and cry for his broken heart,
As I say good-bye to his love I have not yet known.

BETTER THAN BEYOND --YOU

Beyond imagination and before reason,
There is a sensation I want to know.
I want to feel and
Experience to the very depths
Of my inner soul—you.

Beyond sunsets and rainbows,
Nearer to grace but not of this realm,
There's a place I've not yet been.
I have to experience it before I implode
With longing like no other for—you.

Be part of my journey.
Share with me all of this earth and beyond.
Let me taste, feel, smell, touch, and
Breathe all of who you are
Before I die of yearning for—you.

Let me know you, every part of you.
Open your heart to mine and let them beat beside
Each other with a rhythm in total sync,
A body and soul of two like one.
Open to me, and be me--and you.

My Heart And Soul

There is no level beyond the fire within
That smolders brilliant
With white-hot excitement between only us,
Lost in each other.
Completely into me, totally into—you.

No man put asunder what we have found.
No earthly wonder ever touched me so.
I only dreamed of heaven like this feeling
You have given me.
Committed for forever—you.

All of you, my darling, and I give you
All of me,
The burning glow to warm our bodies and our souls forever
And keep us only to each other,
Always wanting more of—you.

Dancing by the silvered light of changing moonglow,
Mark the heart, for here I am,
Looking at the man who treasures my aching heart,
Who mends the world and rights the wind,
My hero—you.

Whispers in the gloomy dark
Make light of frightened nights and lonely places,
Fearing never as forth we go together,
Not alone,
Forever each other's heart and treasure with—you.

Ride the wind, baby, and on the edge,
Let me feel your body swaying with the balance of our beating
hearts.
Fly through this life in awe of that around us,
But more between us,
And forever with each motion felt--with and just for you.

TO SERVE YOU, LORD

From deep within a silent sleep
A whispered voice proclaims of me
To follow

And lulls me gently through the vast
Remaining edges of twilight cast,
And listen,

Hark!

I hear through thought from somewhere
Now unknown.

I feel.

And now I know--
An angel.
The word, my Lord, he gently whispered
And kept me safe through troubled nights.

The angel sent in deep of night
To guide the passage of my dreams.

I tremble.

For until now I was not sure,
But now I know with words from you
Through others sent by you, My Lord.
They speak to me of kinder things.

I hear now, Lord. I saw through blinded eyes.
I saw through deafened ears.

I know.

Your message reached into my soul.

I see.

The angels sent by you to care for such
A wanton being?
To save me, Lord?

I believe.

Truth came gentle from the birth rejoiced
By others,
Often feared
And now my heart swells with love
For You,
For You have led me to the truth.

I trust.

To follow with my heart in footsteps
Always gone before, the others too
Who've come to know Your love.
His humbled heart for You.

Your grace be treasured always now
And service to You I pledge.
For salvation
I rejoice and thank You with my life
And soul to use forever.

And angels always I will watch
And take heed their bidding
To follow You.

Celestial wings of softened down
Light aglow from deep within.
I'll know from You they come to guide
Me through the days spread onto
Earth before me.

Their message I shall heed
And know Your love.

Only through Your grace do I live
To serve You, Lord.

AMEN

I AM READY

Such a fruitful life it's been, learning
lessons presented to me by my loving Father.

The path was sometimes difficult to
Tread, but no matter how weary my feet may
have felt at times, my soul was filled with the joy
of knowing I would be forgiven of my stumbling along the way
and that my journey toward the warm, bright light
would lead me eventually to be with Him, forever.

It's been a good life.

God has blessed me with wondrous gifts, and I have
carried my share of burdens always with
His presence to help me.

Now, as my body grows weary and I know the end of my journey
is growing near, I am filled with excitement and a longing,
for I will soon be home with my Lord and Father. My mortal
life I leave willingly, knowing that immortality with Him
forever awaits me. I celebrate in quiet awe with the knowledge that
eternity will be mine with Him. Jesus gave His life for me
to make this glorious voyage, so that through Him I might be

forgiven of the sins I've committed along the way, yet still go home for eternity with my Father.

I have my treasured memories, but I don't look back now; only forward, as the great light of love and peace draws me closer to His protective care.

I am coming, Father.

Please take me when you're ready for me. Please let me walk with grace and courage as I embrace eternal life in Your care.

I am Yours, and I am ready.

AMEN